Hi, I'm Kasheera Hickson.

I've always had a love for tarot. My fascination with the mystical and spiritual has been with me for as long as I can remember. I got my very first tarot deck when I was around 17—one of the first decks I had was the Osho Zen deck, along with a mini tarot deck that I used to travel with. I've always been intrigued by the idea that cards could somehow provide insight into what's going on in our lives. There was something magical about it, and that curiosity never left me.

So, when the pandemic came around, I found myself in our one-bedroom apartment in sunny Los Angeles, California, like many of us, with more time on my hands to explore my hobbies. Naturally, I felt it was the perfect opportunity to dive deeper into tarot—something I had always wanted to do officially so I could become a tarot reader. I decided to dive into learning tarot, starting with the classic Rider-Waite-Smith deck, using Biddy Tarot's course to get a grip on the meanings of the cards.

But pretty quickly, I realized there was something missing. I wasn't really seeing myself in the cards, and that lack of connection was holding me back from truly understanding and relating to them. I've always been passionate about Photoshop, and I love transforming and painting images. So, I decided to try my hand at recreating the Empress card in my own likeness. The result blew me away. It was beautiful. That was the moment Mahogany Tarot was born.

So, that's how my journey into creating and selling my own tarot deck began. This guide is here to help you navigate that same journey, from concept to creation to successful sales, with a particular focus on the areas where I can offer the most insight: the steps beyond the artwork.

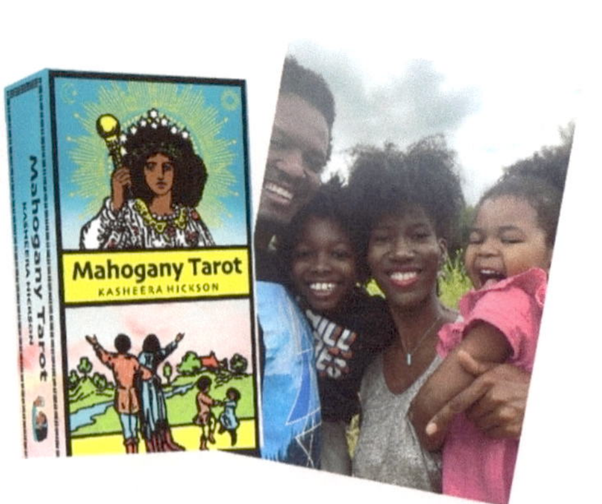

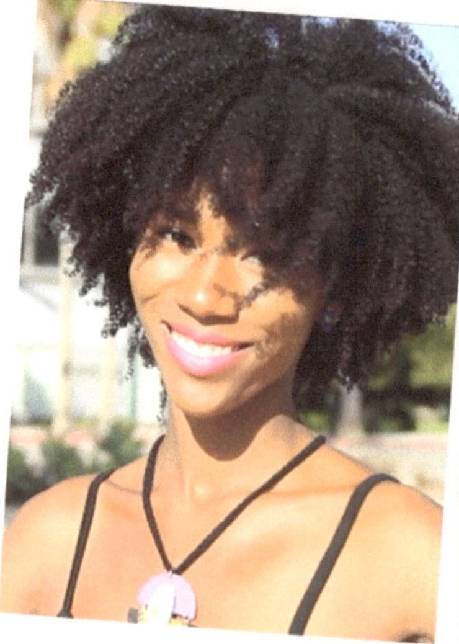

Purpose of This Guide

The purpose of this guide is to help creators take their ideas and dreams from concepts in their minds to actual products in their hands. Too often, we see people creating amazing things, but the process can seem so daunting that it's hard to even know where to start. I want to demystify that process and show you, step-by-step, how it's done, so you can bring your dreams and goals to life.

Representation in the spiritual space is lacking, particularly for people of color. There aren't many decks out there that reflect our experiences, and that needs to change. I want to encourage others to create their projects and get them out into the world. This guide is meant to be a resource that helps you navigate the unknown, showing you that it's all possible, one step at a time.

Concept Development & Artwork Creation

Concept Development

When it came to developing the concept for my tarot deck, I wanted to create something that honored the classic tarot imagery while also bringing a fresh, diverse perspective. My idea was simple: put a diverse spin on the timeless Rider-Waite deck. My concept wasn't overly complex, but it was rooted in a clear vision—one that I felt was missing in the spiritual community.

For those of you who are thinking about creating something completely new or that hasn't been seen before, the first thing I'd recommend is to ask yourself: Is there a demand for it? How does your concept fit into the current landscape of the spiritual community? Are you filling a gap or bringing something unique that people will be excited to have?

It's important to make sure there's a market for your deck because, yes, it's possible to create something amazing that no one ends up buying. That's why figuring out the demand is a crucial step in your concept development. One way to assess demand is by doing a little research. Look at what's already out there. Check platforms like Etsy, Amazon, or tarot communities online to see what's popular and what gaps might exist. If you're creating a niche deck, see how similar niche products are performing. Are there discussions, groups, or forums where people are asking for something like what you're thinking of creating?

Now if your concept was born out of a spark of inspiration, that's something special. Often times, these moments of inspiration are the universe guiding us to step into our purpose.. If you feel deeply called to create it, trust that instinct. Just make sure to also find a way to gauge interest so you can position your deck in a way that resonates with your desired audience..

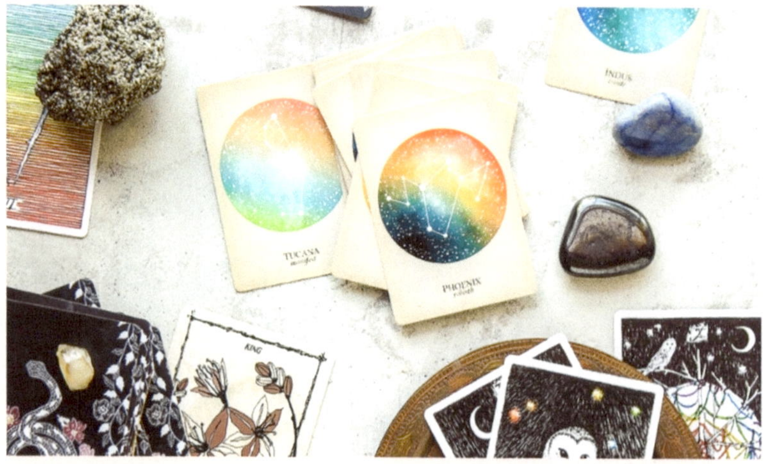

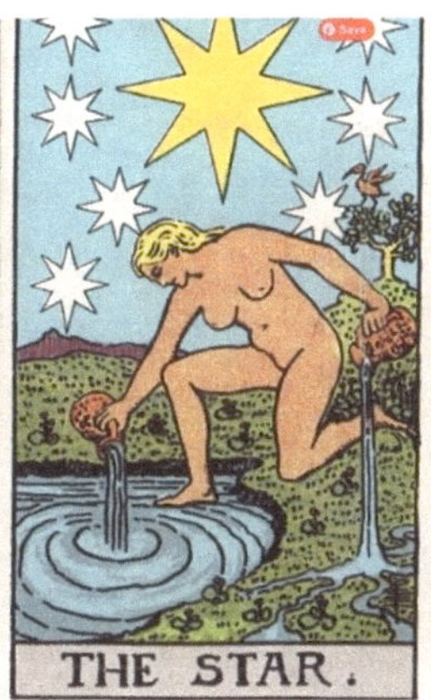

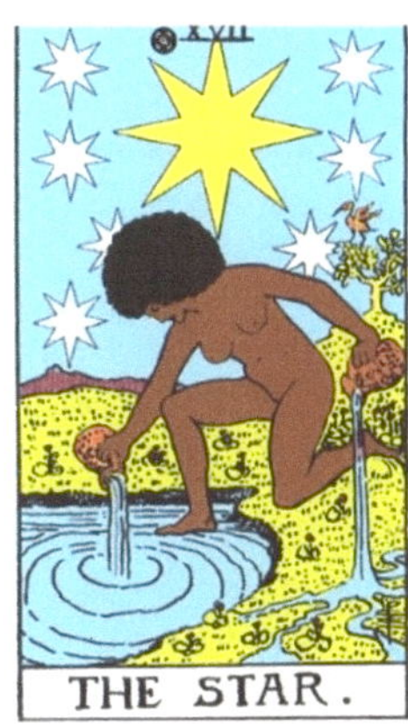

Choosing the Type of Tarot Deck

When deciding on the type of deck I wanted to create, I knew I wanted to stay close to the traditional tarot structure, specifically the Rider–Waite style, because it's what I was most familiar with and what I felt would resonate the most with others. I wasn't interested in creating an oracle deck, though I've since created one as well. The structure and symbolism of the traditional tarot felt like the right framework for me to build upon and infuse with more diversity.

For anyone deciding between creating a traditional tarot deck or something different like an oracle deck, think about what feels most natural to you. If you're drawn to the structure and history of tarot, a traditional deck might be your path. On the other hand, if you want more flexibility or your concept doesn't fit within the confines of traditional tarot, an oracle deck could be the way to go.

Consider what will best serve your vision and your audience. Sometimes it's about what you're passionate about creating, and sometimes it's about what will connect best with the people you're trying to reach.

Artwork Creation

When it came to creating the artwork for my tarot deck, my process was pretty straightforward. I approached each card with the intention of transforming it into a melanated character—someone who reminded me of people in my family or characters I've seen on TV growing up. This personal connection was important to me because I wanted the characters in my deck to feel relatable, especially to other Black people who might not see themselves reflected in traditional tarot decks. As I worked through each card, I found that the images started to take on lives of their own. Even now, when I look at the deck, certain cards remind me of characters from movies like Coming to America or they make me think of my dad. This sense of familiarity and connection was key to making each card unique while also ensuring that the deck resonated with those who might feel underrepresented in the spiritual community.

Artwork Creation

Creating a tarot deck requires the right tools to bring your vision to life, whether you're an experienced digital artist or someone just starting out. Below are some essential digital tools that can help you at various stages of your creative process, each with its own strengths and features to suit different needs.

Photoshop: The All-Around Powerhouse

Photoshop is like the Swiss army knife of digital art. It's a powerful tool for creating, editing, and refining your tarot deck's artwork. Whether you're drawing from scratch, manipulating images, or adding final touches, Photoshop offers a wide range of brushes, filters, and effects that can help you achieve the look you want.

- Best For: Detailed image editing, layering, adding effects, and correcting imperfections.
- Pricing: $10/month for the Adobe Creative Cloud Photography plan, which includes Photoshop.

2. Procreate: The Mobile Artist's Best Friend

If you're an iPad user, Procreate is a must-have. It's an incredibly intuitive app that's perfect for creating hand-drawn artwork. With a wide variety of brushes and tools, Procreate gives you the freedom to draw, paint, and sketch directly on your tablet. It's also great for working on the go, making it a favorite among digital artists.

- Best For: Hand-drawn illustrations, sketching, painting, and creating artwork on the go.
- Pricing: A one-time purchase of around $10.

3. Canva: Design Made Easy

Canva is a user-friendly, drag-and-drop tool that's perfect if you're not a professional designer but still want to create beautiful card layouts and promotional materials. It's especially useful for adding text, creating card borders, and designing marketing materials like social media posts or flyers.

- Best For: Card layouts, adding text and graphics, creating promotional materials.
- Pricing: Free with optional paid features starting at $12.95/month for Canva Pro.

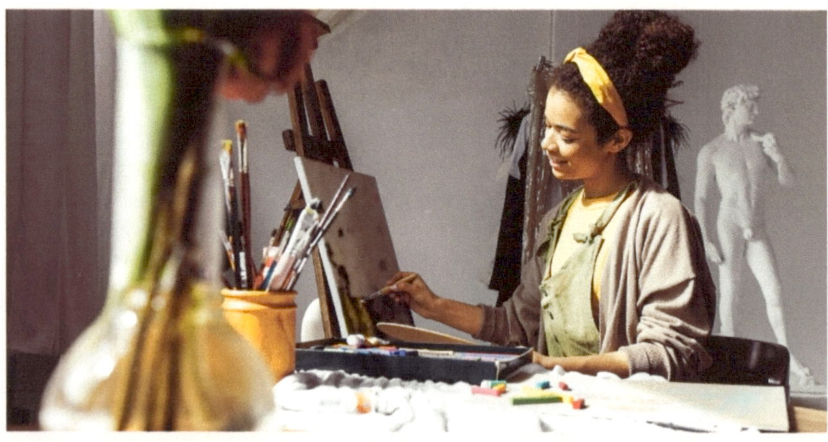

Creation Tools – Continued

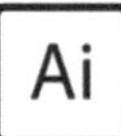

4. Adobe Illustrator: Vector Perfection

For those working with vector graphics, Adobe Illustrator is the go-to tool. It allows you to create artwork that can be scaled infinitely without losing quality. This is particularly useful for designing elements like logos, card back designs, and any intricate details that need to maintain their sharpness at any size.

- Best For: Creating vector images, logos, card back designs, and any scalable graphics.
- Pricing: $20.99/month as part of Adobe Creative Cloud.

5. Affinity Designer: The Affordable Alternative

Affinity Designer offers many of the same features as Adobe Illustrator but at a one-time purchase price, making it a more affordable option for those who need professional-level vector design tools. It's versatile and powerful, perfect for creating high-quality artwork without the ongoing subscription cost.

- Best For: Vector design, scalable artwork, an affordable alternative to Adobe Illustrator.
- Pricing: A one-time purchase of around $55.

6. GIMP: The Free Photoshop Alternative

GIMP (GNU Image Manipulation Program) is an open-source alternative to Photoshop. It's free and offers many of the same features, making it a great option for those on a budget. While it may have a steeper learning curve, it's a powerful tool for editing and creating artwork.

- Best For: Budget-friendly image editing, creating artwork with a variety of tools.
- Pricing: Free.

7. AI Tools: DALL·E and MidJourney

For those looking to integrate AI-generated art into their tarot decks, tools like DALL·E and MidJourney offer unique possibilities. These AI tools can generate artwork based on text prompts, helping you create stunning images quickly. They're particularly useful for generating concepts, creating realistic painted images, and even refining final designs.

- Best For: Quick concept generation, AI-assisted artwork creation, realistic painted images.
- Pricing: DALL·E uses a credit system (e.g., $15 for a set of credits); MidJourney offers subscription plans ranging from $10 to $60/month.

8. FontSquirrel and DaFont: Finding the Perfect Font

Typography is a crucial part of your tarot deck's design. FontSquirrel and DaFont are excellent resources for finding free and paid fonts that can add the perfect touch to your cards. Just make sure to check the licenses for commercial use.

- Best For: Finding and downloading fonts for card titles, guidebooks, and promotional materials.
- Pricing: Many fonts are free, with some premium options available for purchase.

Tips for Using Digital Tools

- **Combine Tools for the Best Results:** Sometimes, the best results come from using multiple tools. For example, you might generate an initial design with AI tools like MidJourney, refine it in Photoshop, and then add text or other elements in Canva or Illustrator.
- **Take Advantage of Tutorials:** Whether you're new to digital art or just exploring a new tool, there are countless tutorials available online. Sites like YouTube or specific design courses can help you get up to speed quickly.
- **Experiment and Have Fun:** Don't be afraid to try new things and experiment with different tools. The creative process is all about exploration, so enjoy it!

My Creation Process

I primarily worked in Photoshop to create the artwork. Since Photoshop is only about $10 a month, I highly recommend getting a subscription and getting familiar with it. Photoshop is incredibly useful for adding elements, tweaking imperfections, and enhancing the overall look of your images. If you're hand-painting your artwork, you might have your own process for making corrections, but you may still need Photoshop—or even Canva—for things like adding titles or text.

If you're new to these tools, watch a few YouTube tutorials to get the basics down. Photoshop has a lot of features that can really enhance your work, and having multiple tools at your disposal as an artist can be a game-changer.

In today's world, AI is becoming more popular, and tools like MidJourney and DALL-E can be used to get inspiration or even create AI-generated decks. Of course, opinions on AI vary, so it's up to you whether you want to incorporate those tools into your process.

When I first started exploring AI tools, the first one I came across was DALL·E. My husband, who's always up-to-date on the latest tech, told me to sign up during their beta phase. As soon as I got in, I became obsessed with how quickly I could bring the ideas in my head to life just by entering a prompt. For me, that meant creating beautiful artwork with Black representation—images of Black families, mothers, fathers, and children that felt personal and culturally rich. DALL·E allowed me to create stunning, realistic, hand-drawn-looking images that I used for my Oracle deck.

One thing I love about DALL·E is how it gives you that realistically painted look, which feels almost like a handcrafted piece of art. The way it handles textures and details is incredible, especially if you're aiming for a traditional, painted style in your tarot deck.

DALL·E Payment Model:

 DALL·E uses a credit system. You can purchase credits (e.g., $15 for a set amount), and each time you generate an image, it uses up some of those credits. I found this model really flexible and cost-effective, especially when you're experimenting with different ideas and generating multiple images.

AI TOOLS Continued

If you're looking for specific styles, there's a tool called Prompt Base where you can purchase prompt codes that help you create exactly the type of artwork you're envisioning, whether it's for children's books, tarot cards, or anything else.

After diving deep into DALL·E, I discovered MidJourney, another AI tool that's fantastic but a bit different in how it operates. MidJourney requires you to use Discord, which might have a bit of a learning curve. You enter your prompt with a command like /imagine, and then you get your generated images.

MidJourney Payment Model:

MidJourney offers several pricing tiers. If you're just playing around, you can go for the basic $10/month plan. But if you're planning to use the images commercially and want them to be private (not visible to everyone on the internet), you'll need the $60/month plan that operates in stealth mode. This is ideal if you're creating something you don't want others to replicate or see until it's ready for the world.

MidJourney vs. DALL·E:

What I really love about MidJourney is how refined and perfect the images come out. They're beautiful, often looking almost too perfect. This can be great depending on the project, but sometimes it might lack the rustic, hand-crafted feel that DALL·E can produce. That said, MidJourney often requires less post-processing, which can save you time if you're looking for a polished final product right away.

Challenges with AI Tools:

One thing to keep in mind with AI tools is that they don't always get everything right—especially when it comes to details like hands and eyes. DALL·E, for example, has a notorious reputation for getting hands wrong. That's where knowing how to use tools like Photoshop comes in handy. I often found myself fixing hands, eyes, or other small imperfections using Photoshop's paint brush tool after generating an image with AI. Having a basic understanding of digital tools can help you tweak and perfect your images, making them truly yours.

Final Thoughts:

AI tools like DALL·E and MidJourney are amazing resources, especially for those who want to create beautiful artwork quickly without necessarily having advanced artistic skills. They open up new possibilities, especially if you're looking to create a tarot deck with a unique style or specific representation. Just remember to experiment, play with the different features, and use them in conjunction with other tools like Photoshop or Canva to achieve the best results.

Finalizing the Artwork

Once the artwork was completed, the final step was to review everything for any imperfections or issues that might have been overlooked. I made sure to go through each card carefully, but I also had a couple of other people take a look at the final artwork. Sometimes, a fresh set of eyes can catch things that you might miss, especially when it comes to designing the box, the back of the box, and any accompanying materials like a booklet. For the booklet, I strongly recommend having someone proofread it for any spelling or grammatical errors. An editor can be incredibly helpful in this process, and there are also AI programs available that can assist with this. I recommend Chat-GPT or Grammarly.

1. **Grammarly: Grammarly** is a popular tool that checks for grammar, spelling, and style issues. It's easy to use and can quickly help you polish your text, making sure everything is error-free and professional.

- Best For: Quick grammar and spelling checks, improving writing style.
- Pricing: Free with optional premium features.

2. **ChatGPT: ChatGPT** can be a great resource for more than just text generation. You can use it to review and refine your writing, asking it to check for errors, suggest improvements, or even help rephrase sentences for clarity.

- Best For: Text refinement, grammar and spelling checks, generating alternative wording.
- Pricing: Free with options for paid subscriptions.

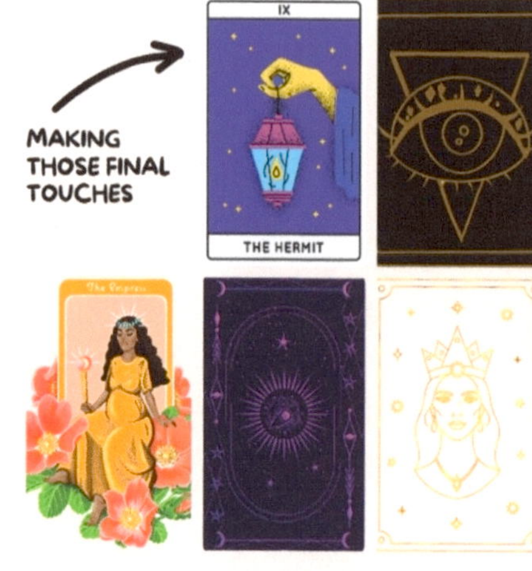

REVIEWING YOUR ARTWORK

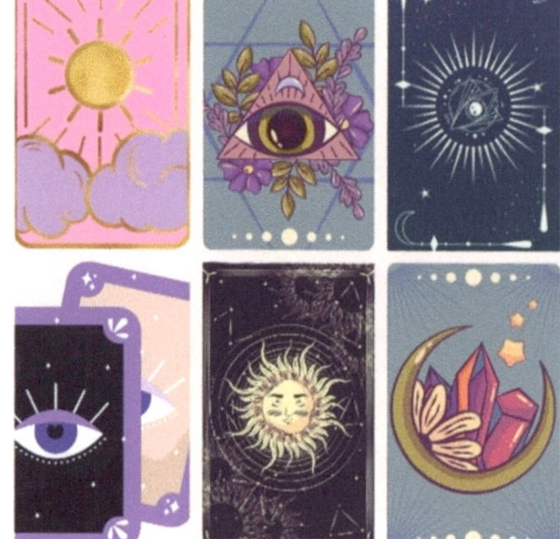

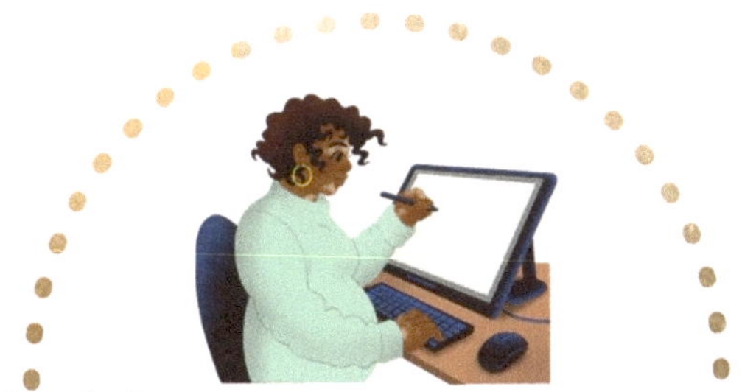

Working with an Artist

For those of you who aren't creating the artwork yourself and plan to hire an artist, it's important to find someone who can bring your vision to life. There are plenty of great websites where you can find artists for hire, including:

1. **Upwork** - A popular platform where you can find freelancers, including graphic designers and artists. You can post your project and review proposals from artists all over the world.
2. **Behance** - A network of creative professionals where you can explore portfolios and directly contact artists who match your style and vision.
3. **Fiverr** - Another platform where you can hire freelance artists. It's easy to find artists based on budget, and many offer tarot-specific design services.

When contacting an artist, find out how they charge—whether it's per image, a flat fee for the entire deck, or an hourly rate. It's crucial to have a good rapport and clear communication with your artist. Make sure they fully understand your vision. It's a good idea to have them create a sample image based on your ideas before committing to the full project. This way, you'll know if they can execute your vision in a way that feels true to what you want to achieve.

Little White Booklet and/or Companion Book

Including a Little White Booklet (LWB) with your deck can add a lot of value, especially for beginners. Whether you choose to go digital or print, make sure the content is clear and easy to follow. Your LWB doesn't have to be long, but it should provide enough guidance for someone to use your deck confidently.

If you're thinking about writing a companion book, it's a great way to dive deeper into the meanings of the cards or the theme of your deck. You can offer card spreads, detailed interpretations, or even your own experiences with the deck. This can be especially appealing to customers who want to explore your deck in greater depth. And remember, the formatting matters—consider things like font size and layout to ensure that your book is as user-friendly as possible. Some creators opt out of creating a little white book and let their customers read the deck intuitively - its up to you to decide what makes sense for your deck but don't be afraid to ask the people you trust whether they think your deck needs a guidebook or not. My little white book has stuck to the basics like keyword meanings for reversed and upright positions as well as briefly covering symbols, colors, numerology, and timing.

The Manufacturing Process

Finding a Manufacturer

When it came time to find a manufacturer for my tarot deck, I started with a basic Google search for print-on-demand printers specifically for tarot decks. There are a several options out there, including Shuffle Ink, Make Playing Cards, WJPC, and Print Ninja, which is the one I ultimately chose.

I found Print Ninja through a Google search and decided to order their sample pack to get a feel for the different card stocks they offered. I also reached out to them with a few questions, and they were quick to respond, which I really appreciated. Once I used their quote calculator and started communication with them, they assigned me a dedicated person to help bring my product to life. Having that direct line of communication with someone who could guide me through the process really sealed the deal for me, and that's why I went with Print Ninja.

If you're looking for a manufacturer, I recommend researching multiple options and reaching out to them to ask questions. Order samples if you can, and consider how responsive they are. Having someone you can easily communicate with can make the whole process much smoother.

The cost of manufacturing your deck can vary greatly depending on the choices you make, such as the type of box, any specialty finishes, and other customizations.

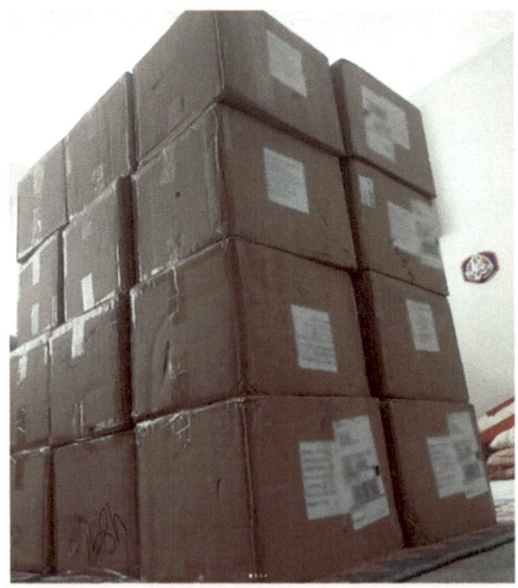

My first 1000 decks

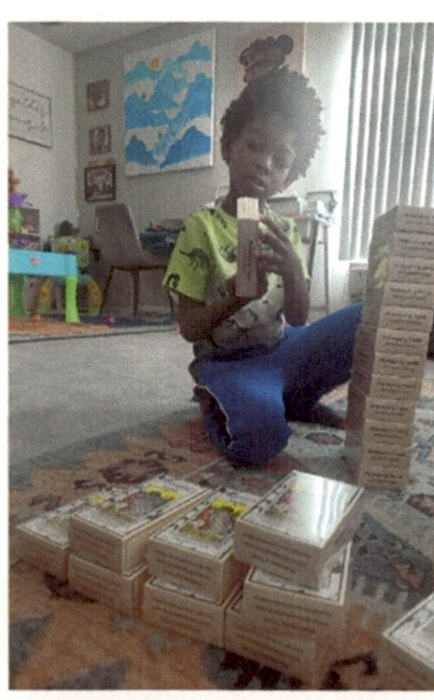

My sonshine inspecting each deck!

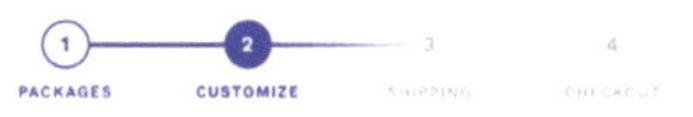

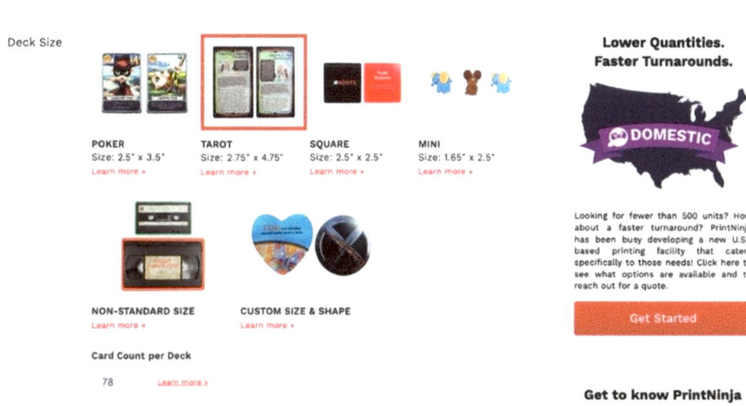

Using PrintNinja's Calculator Tool:

One of the tools I found extremely helpful during this process is PrintNinja's calculator tool. This online tool allows you to input all the specific details you want for your deck, such as:

- **Box Type:** Whether you want a tuck box, two-part box, or a magnetic closure box, the calculator will show you how each option affects the overall cost.
- **Specialty Finishes:** If you're considering adding special touches like gold foil stamping or metallic accents, the calculator can estimate how much these will add to your production costs. These enhancements can significantly increase your total cost, sometimes by $1,000 to $2,000 or more, depending on the size of your print run and the type of finish.
- **Gilded Edges:** For certain customizations, like gilded edges, you might need to reach out directly to PrintNinja (or your chosen manufacturer) to get an accurate quote, as not all options are available in the calculator.

Physical Rough Copy vs. PDF Proof:

PrintNinja, like many manufacturers, offers the option to receive either a PDF proof or a physical rough copy of your deck before full production begins. While a PDF proof can give you a sense of layout and design, I strongly recommend investing in a physical rough copy. Here's why:

- Color Accuracy: A physical proof lets you see exactly how the colors will appear on the final product. If there's a discrepancy when the full order arrives, you can compare it to your rough copy and provide photographic evidence to the manufacturer if needed.
- Tactile Experience: Holding a physical proof in your hands allows you to experience the deck the way your customers will, giving you confidence in the final product's quality and feel.
- Issue Resolution: If there are any issues with the final production, having a physical proof as a reference can be crucial in negotiating with the manufacturer for corrections or refunds.

Cost Considerations:

While the physical proof is an additional cost—often quite expensive—it's a vital part of ensuring that your final product meets your expectations. Even if you've created a prototype using a service like MakePlayingCards, the physical proof from your main manufacturer will be different and more indicative of the final product's quality.

Sourcing and Working with Overseas Manufacturers: The Alibaba Experience

Another option that some creators explore is using companies like Alibaba for manufacturing their tarot decks. This can be a viable route, especially if you're looking for competitive pricing. However, it's crucial to ensure that you feel comfortable with their communication style. Clear communication is key to making sure that both you and the manufacturer understand each other's expectations.

Alibaba allows you to look at reviews, star ratings, and gold sellers, which can help you find a reputable manufacturer. I've personally used Alibaba to order tarot cloth bags that I include with each order as a little bonus for my customers—people love bonuses, and it was a great deal.

Alibaba, as well as AliExpress, can also be excellent sources for getting other bulk items like crystals if you want to include extra goodies with your deck.

If you decide to go with a Chinese printer or a printer based outside of the U.S., it's important to ask about receiving a sample of their card stocks and examples of other decks they've printed. You want to ensure that the quality meets your standards before committing to a large order.

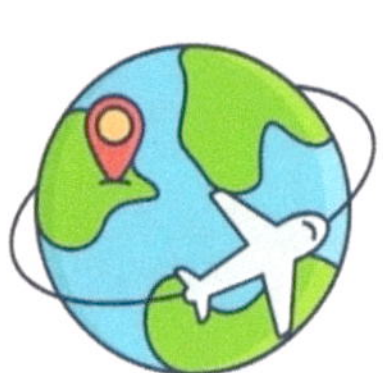

Printing Your Artwork 

Printing your deck is where things can get technical, but it's also where the magic happens! You've spent all this time creating your artwork, so you want to make sure it prints beautifully. Pay attention to the DPI (dots per inch) resolution of your digital files—300 DPI is standard for high-quality printing. Also, be aware of the color mode; printers typically use CMYK, so if you've been working in RGB, you'll want to convert your files.

Here's a step-by-step guide to help you prepare your files correctly, primarily focusing on Photoshop but also providing alternative tools if you're using other software.

1. Preparing Your Files in Photoshop:

Photoshop is a powerful tool that allows you to create and prepare print-ready files with precision. Here's what you need to know

Color Mode: CMYK: 

- Most manufacturers, including PrintNinja, require your images to be in CMYK color mode. CMYK stands for Cyan, Magenta, Yellow, and Key (Black), which is the color model used in printing. This ensures that the colors in your final printed deck will be accurate.
  - **How to Convert to CMYK:**
  - In Photoshop, you can convert your files to CMYK by going to Image > Mode > CMYK Color. Make sure to check your colors after conversion, as they may appear slightly different than they did in RGB mode.

Resolution: 300 DPI: 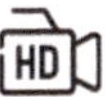

- Your images should be set to 300 DPI (Dots Per Inch) to ensure that they are high enough quality for printing. This resolution provides the necessary detail and sharpness in the printed cards.
  - Setting DPI in Photoshop:
  - When you create your document or check your existing file, go to Image > Image Size and ensure that the resolution is set to 300 pixels/inch.

Organizing Files:

- Once all your images are prepared, organize them into folders. For example, you might have one folder for the card images and another for the booklet files. After organizing, compress these folders into a ZIP file, which makes it easier to upload them to your manufacturer's platform.

Uploading Files:

- After preparing and organizing your files, upload them according to your manufacturer's guidelines. Typically, you'll upload your ZIP files to their designated platform.

Requesting and Using Box Templates:

If your deck includes a custom box, such as a tuck box, two-part box, or magnetic closure box, you'll need to request a specific template from your manufacturer. This template will ensure that your artwork fits perfectly on the box design.

Requesting a Template:

Contact your manufacturer and ask them to provide you with the template for the box you've chosen. They will send you a file that includes the exact dimensions and guides for where to place your designs.

Applying Your Artwork to the Template:

Open the template in Photoshop or your preferred design software and add your artwork. Make sure that all elements fit within the designated areas on the template to avoid any issues with the final product.

Shrink Wrapping Option:

Consider requesting that your manufacturer shrink-wrap your deck. Shrink wrapping protects the deck during shipping, especially from environmental factors like moisture. It's a small addition that can make a big difference in maintaining the quality of your product.

ISBN Number

Since I have also created childrens books I did purchase an ISBN through Bowker.com for my deck. I also used a site "Kindlepreneur" to convert that ISBN number to a barcode that I can put on the back of the deck box design for free. This has been very helpful for platforms like Amazon that may require it.

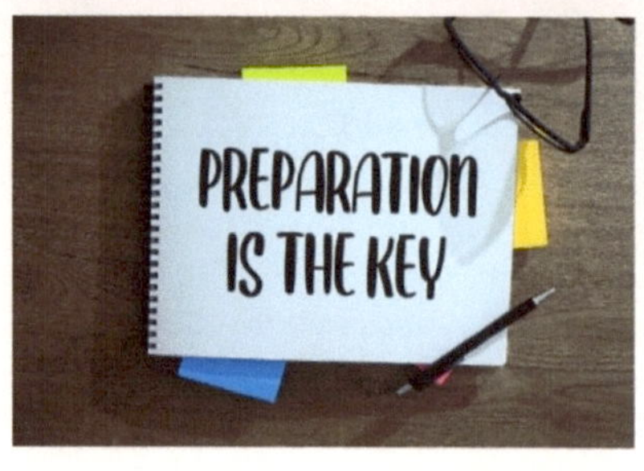

Alternative Tools for Preparing Artwork:

If you're not using Photoshop, there are several other tools you can use to prepare your files for print:

Procreate is excellent for creating hand-drawn artwork directly on your iPad. After completing your design, you can export your files in CMYK color mode and at 300 DPI. Use Procreate for creating initial artwork and then finalize it in another program like Photoshop or Affinity Designer.

Canva is a user-friendly tool that allows you to create designs and export them in print-ready formats. However, Canva's color mode is RGB, so you might need to convert files to CMYK in another tool if your manufacturer requires it. Canva is best for adding text, borders, and creating card layouts.

Affinity Designer is a vector-based design tool similar to Adobe Illustrator. It allows you to work in CMYK and export print-ready files. It's a powerful alternative to Photoshop, especially for creating vector elements like logos and card back designs.

GIMP is a free alternative to Photoshop. It supports CMYK with additional plugins and can handle high-resolution images. GIMP is suitable for users who need a budget-friendly option without sacrificing too much functionality.

Final Checklist Before Printing:

Checklist:

Double-Check File Specifications:

Ensure that all files meet the manufacturer's specifications, including CMYK color mode, 300 DPI resolution, and correct dimensions.

Proof Your Files:

Before submitting, proofread any text and double-check your images for any errors or adjustments that might be needed. Use tools like Grammarly or ChatGPT for text checks, and have someone else review your files if possible.

Confirm with Manufacturer:

After uploading your files, confirm with your manufacturer that everything is in order. They might provide a PDF proof or physical rough copy to review before proceeding with the full print run.

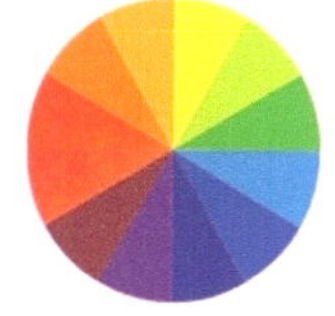

Cardstock:

Another thing to consider is the card stock. The feel of the cards in someone's hand can make a big difference. I usually go with 350 GSM because it's sturdy but not too thick. And when it comes to the finish, whether you choose matte or glossy, it's all about how you want the cards to feel and look Glossy may show more fingerprints as well as make the cards too slippery so its best to order a physical proof you can play around with..

Color Variance:

When it came to manufacturing, the first batch of 1,000 decks turned out great with only a few minor details that I missed. However, in the second batch of 2,500 decks, I encountered issues with color consistency. Some decks had browns that were too orange or too dark, which didn't match the rough copy I had approved. This is why it's so important to pay for a rough copy, even though it's expensive. It allows you to catch these issues early and potentially get a refund or have the manufacturer redo the batch.

Protecting Your Artwork

When working with manufacturers, especially those overseas, you need to be cautious about protecting your artwork. Unfortunately, there have been cases where deck creators have found knockoff versions of their decks being sold without their permission.

To safeguard your work, you might want to consider having the manufacturer sign a Non-Disclosure Agreement (NDA) or a contract that explicitly states that they cannot reproduce or share your designs. This can help protect your intellectual property and give you some legal standing if issues arise.

Another way to protect your artwork is by registering it with copyright authorities in your country. This can give you additional legal protection if your designs are copied without permission. Make sure you have all agreements in writing and take steps to protect your intellectual property from the start.

Finalizing Design – Continued

Cultural Sensitivity

When creating a tarot deck, especially one that draws on diverse cultures or uses traditional symbols, it's super important to be mindful of cultural sensitivity. You want to make sure that you're honoring the cultures you're representing rather than appropriating them. This means doing your research and maybe even consulting with people from the culture you're depicting to make sure you're getting it right.

Finalizing the Design

Once I placed the order with Print Ninja, the process of finalizing the design began. I'm not going to lie—the first time I ordered a deck, I used a credit card. If you're considering this route, I suggest using a card with a 0% interest promotion for at least 12 to 15 months. This gives you time to get your decks, start selling, and hopefully pay off the card before interest kicks in. You could also look into balance transfer deals to avoid paying more in interest.

Other ways to finance your project include crowdfunding through platforms like Kickstarter, getting help from family and friends, or seeking a small business loan or grant.

Once I placed my order, I spent a lot of time going back and forth with Print Ninja to tweak small details. Even though I ordered in February, it took about three months of adjustments before the decks were ready to ship. My advice? Only place your order when your artwork is as close to finalized as possible. This will help avoid delays and keep things moving smoothly.

The process of finalizing the design involved constant communication and adjustments. Print Ninja was patient with every change I made, sending me new proofs each time until I was satisfied with how everything looked. Once I gave the final approval, the decks were moved into production and took about 3 months to arrive.

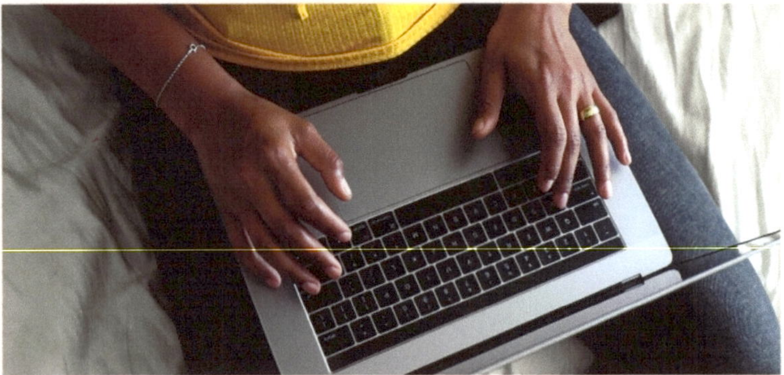

Finalizing Design – Continued

Pricing and Budgeting

Pricing your deck can be tricky, and it's something I learned the hard way. For my first deck, I ordered 1,000 copies, and after calculating the total cost—including shipping materials and everything that went into the packaging—the cost per deck was about $5.80. I initially priced the deck at $29.99, which I now realize might have been a bit of a newbie mistake.

While the price point made the decks more affordable and likely contributed to high sales, once Etsy took their fees and I subtracted the production costs, the profit margins were pretty slim. Now, I've priced my deck at $49.99, but I often run sales, so the average customer is paying between $35 and $40. My priority is to keep the decks moving rather than having them sit unsold, so I adjust the price as needed to ensure I'm still making a good profit margin.

When it comes to pricing your deck, you'll want to consider the total cost of production, including shipping and packaging. A common formula is to take your total costs and multiply by at least 2.5 to 3 times to ensure you're covering your expenses and making a profit. However, pricing can vary based on your market, competition, and how much profit you want to make. Ideally, you want to aim for a profit margin of at least 50% or more, but this can depend on your business goals and costs.

If you're struggling with pricing, consider the value of your deck—handmade or indie decks often command a higher price because of their uniqueness and the work that goes into them. Don't be afraid to charge what your product is worth. You can look on sites like Etsy to see what other creators have set their price at and price your deck competitively. Main stream traditionally published decks are much cheaper - you could go that route as well. Currently I only have experience with self publishing my deck.

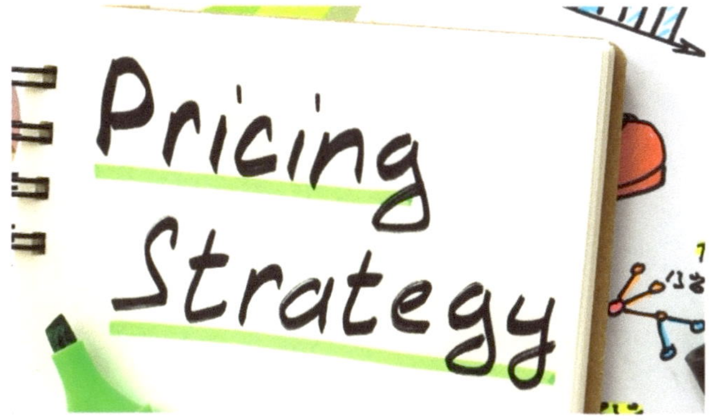

Marketing and Selling Your Deck

Setting Up Online Stores

When I first started selling my tarot deck, I began with Etsy. I did have a WordPress website at the time, but due to some issues with my hosting company, I eventually switched to Shopify. So, my primary sales channels became Etsy and my Shopify website. Later on, I also added my deck to Amazon, but I found that Amazon was the most complex platform to navigate. It's not as intuitive as Etsy, and the listing process can be a bit more challenging.

For beginners, I definitely recommend starting with Etsy. It's easy to set up your first listing and your store, and it's a great way to get your product in front of potential customers quickly. My deck started selling on Etsy fairly quickly—within two weeks of posting. If you want to test the waters and gauge interest, you could start with a small batch, maybe ten decks from a print-on-demand service like Make Playing Cards, and list them at a lower price just to see how people respond.

If you're ready to expand beyond Etsy, having your own website is crucial. Shopify is a good option for setting up your own online store, and it integrates well with other sales channels but it is pretty expensive per year. Consider other options if you are working with a smaller budget like Wix, Squarespace, and Wordpress/WooCommerce. Be sure to secure your brand website name through a registrar like godaddy.com which is my go to option.

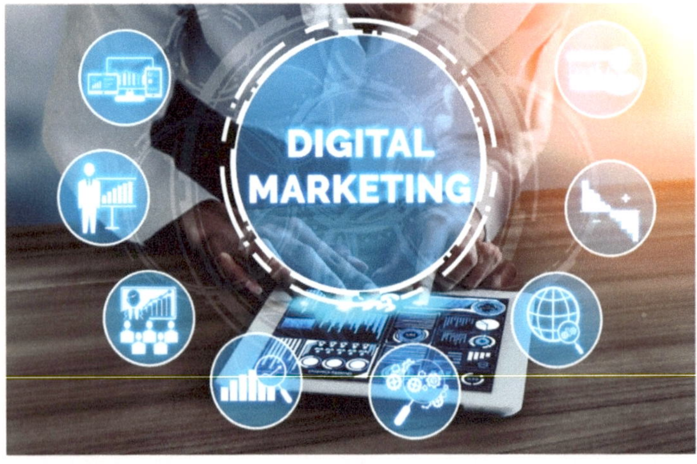

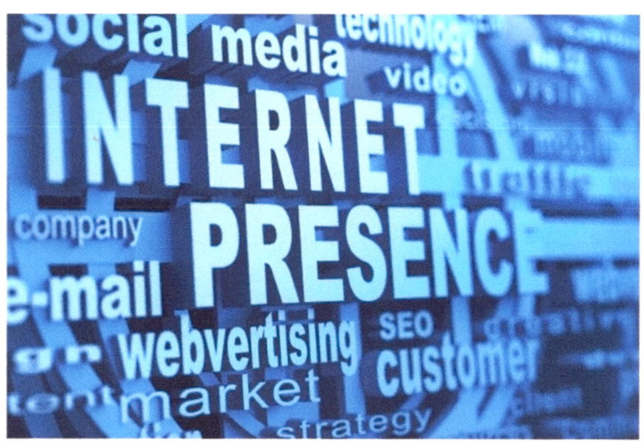

Building an Online Presence

Building an online presence is key to driving traffic to your store and growing your brand. I secured all my social media handles under my brand name and started creating content that showcased my deck. Since my product is a tarot deck, I focused on Instagram, where I posted content like unboxing videos, explanations of card meanings, behind-the-scenes looks at how I pack and ship orders, and new deck reveals.

The goal is to create as much content as possible once you have a copy of your deck in hand. Show it off in different ways, and make it visually appealing. Use tools like ChatGPT to help you come up with a social media marketing plan—there's so much available to you that can help streamline your efforts. Before launching my deck, I also researched YouTubers and tarot readers who I thought would be a good fit to send my deck to for free. Influencer marketing has proven to be incredibly effective for me. When people with a following start unboxing and talking about your product, it creates a buzz and excitement around your deck.

I'm still learning about other forms of marketing, like getting featured in blogs or holiday gift guides, but influencer marketing has been a great start. If you're looking to expand your reach, consider PR efforts that could get your product featured in these types of spaces.

 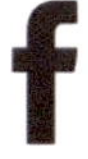  

Marketing and Sales Strategies

Marketing your deck is where you really get to have some fun, but it's also where strategy comes into play. Beyond just posting on social media, think about how you can create a buzz around your deck. Collaborating with influencers who align with your brand can be a game-changer. Reach out to tarot readers who are popular on YouTube or Instagram and see if they'd be interested in reviewing your deck. It's also worth putting together a media kit—a simple PDF that includes images of your deck, your story, and key points about why your deck is unique.

Running a SWOT analysis (Strengths, Weaknesses, Opportunities, Threats) can help you figure out where you stand in the market and what areas you need to focus on. And don't forget about email marketing—it's a great way to keep in touch with people who are already interested in your deck and to let them know about new releases or special offers.

Finally, when sales slow down, don't panic. Every business has ups and downs. Instead, use that time to reassess your strategy. Maybe run a special promotion or create some fresh content to re-engage your audience. Always have a plan for these moments because they will happen, and how you respond can make all the difference.

Product Launch and Ongoing Sales

To keep sales consistent over time, the most important thing I focus on is SEO (Search Engine Optimization). Making sure the keywords in your listing, description, and titles are what your target customers are searching for is crucial. Too often, people title their products based on what sounds good to them, but it's not necessarily what customers are searching for.

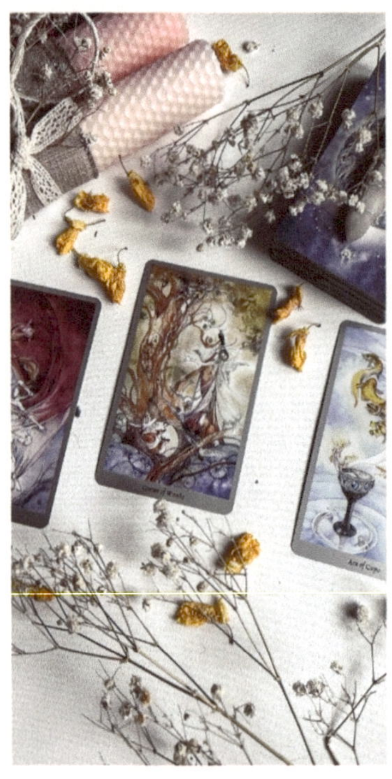

There are tools like eRank, Everbee, and Google Keyword Planner that can help you find the top keywords in your category. You'll need at least the top 20 keywords that aren't oversaturated or overused on the platform you're using.

During slow periods, I also keep my social media active and adjust my pricing strategy to keep products moving. Running sales or promotions can help boost sales when things slow down. The key is to keep your deck in front of potential customers, whether through consistent social media activity, optimized listings, or sales events.

CHAPTER FOUR

Customer Experience and Feedback

Customer Engagement

One of the biggest things I do that customers really appreciate is include a handwritten thank you card with each order. It's my way of showing genuine appreciation for their support and letting them know how much it means to me that they chose my deck. This little gesture adds a personal touch that you just don't get with a standard purchase from a big retailer like Amazon. It's an important part of building that connection with my customers.

For print-on-demand items, such as those created through platforms like Printify, Printful, Guten, or Printed Mint, I always send a follow-up thank you email. In that email, I let them know that their item will be shipped by our production partner and provide a timeline for when they can expect it to arrive. If they've ordered multiple items that might arrive separately—like a deck and a shirt—I make sure to mention that they can expect two packages. This helps avoid any confusion or worry if one item arrives before the other. Print-on-demand lets you have your tarot card designs printed on items like shirts and mugs by a company, which produces and ships them directly to your customers when ordered.

Handling Customer Feedback

Customer feedback is crucial, and I make sure to address it promptly, whether it's positive or negative. If a customer contacts me about a missing order, I'm quick to respond and investigate the issue. I might ask them to check with their building's front desk or around their apartment complex if the package was left somewhere unexpected. My goal is always to reassure the customer that I'm on top of the situation.

On Etsy, I don't allow refunds, but Amazon's policies are different, and they do allow customers to return items even after they've been opened. That's why I think making a quality product is so important—it reduces the chances of returns. If something goes missing or is lost in transit, Amazon covers the refund if you purchase shipping through them, which is a great safety net. On Etsy, though, I generally send a replacement if a package goes missing, even though it means absorbing the cost of the product and reshipping. It's rare, but it does happen, and offering this level of customer service helps maintain positive reviews.

Sometimes, despite my no-refunds policy on Etsy, I'll make an exception. For instance, I had a customer who felt that the deck didn't sit well with her spirit and requested a refund. I chose to honor her request, even though it's not my usual practice. If these situations are rare, it's often better to just resolve them and avoid negative energy or reviews.

Handling Customer Feedback Continued

Regarding feedback on the product itself, card stock quality is something people often comment on. I use 350 GSM card stock, which I find to be a great balance between durability and ease of shuffling. Some customers might still find it too thin, but overall, most people love how my cards shuffle. That's why it's crucial to thoroughly test your rough copy—make sure the cards feel good in your hands, spread well, and meet your quality standards because customers will definitely notice and comment on these details.

Handling Complaints

If you get a return or a complaint, try to resolve it in a way that leaves the customer feeling heard and respected. Sometimes this might mean giving a refund or sending a replacement, even if it's not strictly necessary. It's about protecting your brand's reputation in the long run. And yes, there might be times when you have to deal with angry or difficult customers. It's not fun, but staying calm and courteous is crucial.

Also, don't be afraid to ask for reviews or feedback. Even if the feedback isn't glowing, it gives you a chance to improve and shows that you care about your customers' experiences.

Building Community

Building a strong community around your brand starts with delivering a solid product and providing excellent customer service. I've found that exceeding customer expectations, whether it's with the quality of the product or the speed of shipping, can really help generate positive feedback and repeat customers. I also try to maintain an active presence on social media and keep my customers engaged with regular updates, new content, and behind-the-scenes looks at my process. This helps build a sense of community and keeps customers connected to my brand.

Ultimately, everything begins with making a quality product. If you focus on that, everything else—customer satisfaction, positive reviews, and a loyal community—will naturally follow.

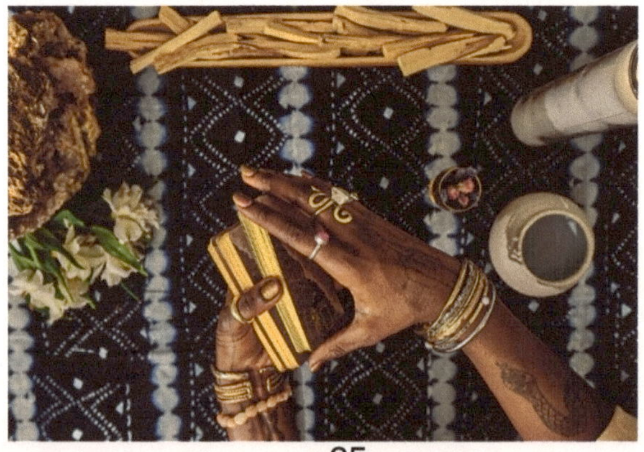

Scaling and Expanding Your Business

Expanding Product Lines

Expanding beyond just tarot decks has been an exciting part of growing my business. Using print-on-demand companies like Printify, Printful, Guten, and Printed Mint, I've been able to offer a wide range of products featuring my tarot card designs. Some of the most popular items include t-shirts, stickers for journaling, mugs, sweatshirts, and candles—people love candles! I've also added keychains, fleece blankets, and even woven blankets. Surprisingly, blankets have been a big hit.

When expanding your product line, I recommend sticking with items that people commonly enjoy showcasing, like apparel and home goods. Take a look at the catalogs offered by these print-on-demand companies to see the variety of products you can create. However, be mindful of pricing your products correctly to ensure a good profit margin. Remember, you'll often need to cover the cost of these orders before receiving payment, so make sure you have the funds available.

If your deck is consistently selling, it's a good sign that you're ready to expand. Use customer feedback as a guide—many of my product expansions came directly from customer requests. For instance, I've added a mini version of my deck, a gold gilded edge version, and keychains based on what customers were asking for.

Wholesale and Retail Opportunities

To expand into wholesale, I started using a site called FAIRE which is a marketplace where retailers look for products to buy in bulk. I've made some great sales through FAIR, and it's been a fantastic way to reach new customers. I also directly reach out to brick-and-mortar stores, specifically targeting physical locations to avoid too much competition in the online space.

My first wholesale deal was with House of Intuition, where they purchased 100 decks for their multiple stores. If you're considering wholesale, craft a strong outreach email and set aside time to focus on reaching out to potential retail partners. Wholesale orders can be substantial, so always ship them via priority mail to ensure tracking. I once had a wholesale order of 10 decks that got lost in the mail because the label was cut off, and it couldn't be returned to me. So, make sure your full address is on the label and that everything is printed correctly.

International Sales

Selling internationally has opened up my business to markets I never expected. I've shipped my decks to places like Japan, Greece, France, Canada, and Switzerland. Expanding internationally can bring in more customers, but it also comes with its own set of challenges.

I prefer using USPS for international orders because their fees are usually lower and more manageable for customers. I had one challenging experience shipping to Canada through UPS where the duties and taxes were unexpectedly high, which upset the customer. They felt they should have been informed of these costs upfront, but as sellers, we don't always know what a country will charge.

Etsy allows you to set up international shipping easily, and it even provides instructions on how to handle international orders. However, instead of using Etsy's Global Post, which can be slow, I use Pirate Ship for faster shipping times. Offering your products internationally is definitely worth considering—you might find that your concept resonates even more in other countries.

To ensure accurate shipping costs, get the correct weight of your product and let the platform calculate the pricing for you. Don't be afraid to open up your shop to international markets—you might be surprised at the demand from around the world.

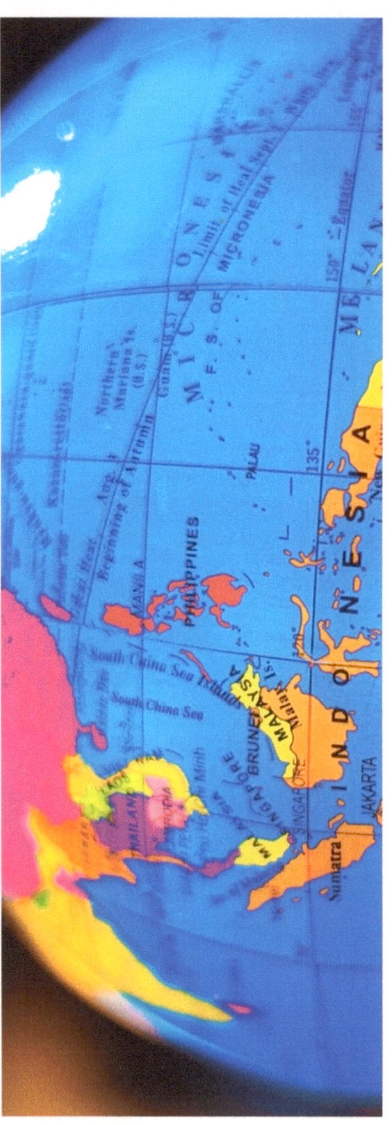

Managing Finances and Inventory

Financial Management

When it comes to financial management, I rely heavily on Excel spreadsheets, specifically those you can purchase on Etsy. These spreadsheets are designed to help you track all your expenses, profits, and other financial details, breaking everything down so that when it's time to do taxes or meet with your tax preparer, all the information is organized and ready. I love using these spreadsheets because they keep everything in one place and make the whole process much easier.

For my business banking, I set up a business checking account with Wells Fargo, where all my business deposits go. I also use business credit cards for all my business purchases, which helps me earn points and enjoy perks from those cards. My favorite business credit card right now is the American Express Blue Card. Additionally, I have a business line of credit with Wells Fargo, which has been really useful. If you're looking for financing options, I also recommend checking out credit unions like Navy Federal Credit Union—they often offer better deals on interest rates and other financial products.

While I've used QuickBooks in the past and it's a great option, I personally prefer sticking with my spreadsheets for now. They keep me organized and are easier for me to manage on a daily basis.

Inventory Management

For inventory management, I keep things simple and track everything by hand in a notebook. Every couple of months, I'll do an inventory update, counting what I have left and making sure to account for any decks I'm sending to influencers. This manual method works for me, but it's important to stay on top of it to avoid overstocking or running out of product.

Speaking of overstocking, I made the mistake of ordering 2,500 decks in my second order when I probably could have gotten by with just 1,000. While ordering in bulk can save money per unit, it also means you might end up with more inventory than you can sell in a reasonable amount of time. This can lead to having to run sales or significantly lower prices just to move the inventory, which can cut into your profits.

Inventory Management Continued

If you find yourself in a situation where you've overstocked and inventory isn't moving fast enough, there are a few strategies you can consider:

- Promotions and Bundles: Create promotions or bundle products together to offer more value and encourage customers to buy.
- Limited-Time Offers: Use scarcity by offering limited-time discounts to create urgency.
- Wholesale Offers: Reach out to retailers or wholesalers who might be interested in purchasing your inventory in bulk.
- Online Marketplaces: Consider listing excess inventory on different online marketplaces or platforms where you might reach a different audience.

Budgeting and Planning

Programs like ChatGPT can also be really helpful when you're trying to develop a business plan or set up a budget. The ability to brainstorm and get advice quickly can save a lot of time.

At the end of the year, I do my own taxes, and having everything organized in spreadsheets makes that process much smoother. I highly recommend using similar tools to keep your finances in order from the start—it will save you a lot of headaches later on.

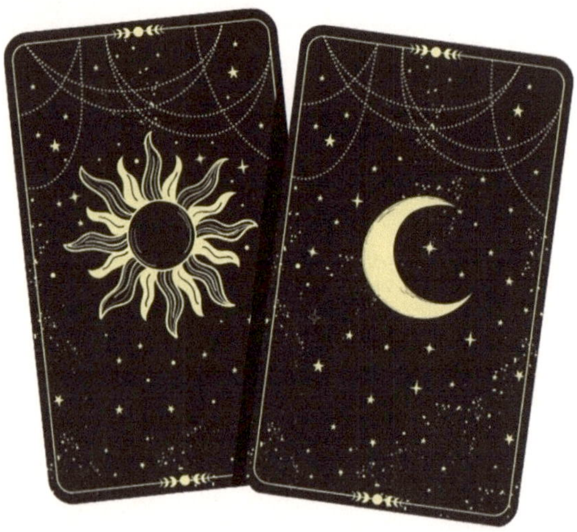

Navigating Challenges

Overcoming Obstacles

One of the biggest challenges I've faced in my tarot business is maintaining consistent sales, especially as more competitors have entered the market. When I first started, there weren't many black tarot decks or decks with black representation on Etsy, but now the market is more saturated. This increased competition means I have to stay on top of my SEO, making sure my keywords and everything are in line with what people are really searching for so that they can still find my product through all the new listings popping up.

There have been times when I've made mistakes, like changing a bestseller listing on Etsy. They say if you have a bestseller, you shouldn't do too much editing to that particular listing, and I learned that the hard way. Making changes affected its visibility, and my sales took a hit. Also, increasing the price without fully understanding my customer base led to a drop in sales. I've had to find that sweet spot where customers feel like they're getting a good value without feeling like they're paying too much.

When my Etsy sales slowed down, I had to think on my toes. I started focusing more on Amazon, improving my SEO there, and that helped boost my sales to make up for the dip on Etsy. This experience taught me not to be too dependent on one platform—selling wherever you can, whether it's through events, online platforms, or social media ads, is important.

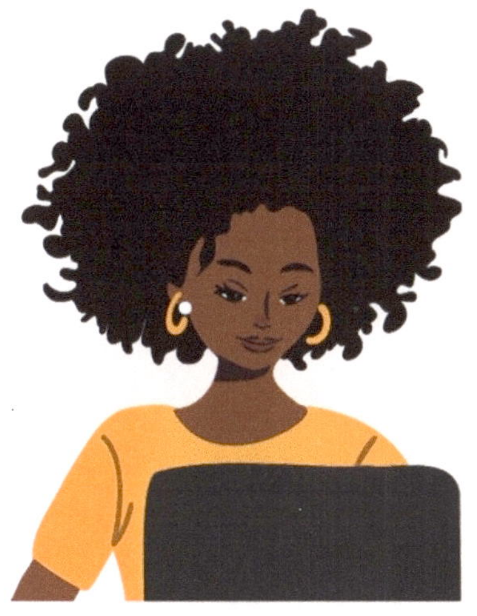

Adapting to Change

The market for black tarot decks and spiritual products has grown, which is exciting but also challenging. I've had to adapt by staying on top of trends and being flexible in my approach. When new competitors or trends emerge, I look at how I can incorporate them into my strategy without losing sight of what makes my brand unique.

If you find yourself in a similar situation, remember to stay informed about changes in your field and be willing to pivot when necessary. It's all about finding creative ways to keep your product relevant and visible.

Self Care

Running a business, especially a creative one, can be emotionally and mentally taxing. It's so important to take care of your mental health throughout the process. There will be moments when you feel overwhelmed or burnt out, and that's okay. The key is to recognize those feelings and take time to recharge.

Whether it's stepping away for a day, meditating, or just doing something that brings you joy outside of work, self-care is essential. Remember, your business will be stronger if you're taking care of yourself. Don't be afraid to set boundaries, whether that's with customers, your work hours, or even your own expectations. It's easy to fall into the trap of thinking you have to do everything all at once, but pacing yourself is crucial for long-term success.

Staying Motivated

What keeps me motivated is knowing that I've created something that I really wanted to see in the world and seeing other people appreciate it as well. It's amazing to receive positive feedback, especially when customers notice the quality and dedication I put into the product. That recognition keeps me going.

I also feel a deep sense of purpose in wanting to see more diversity in the spiritual space. I've often thought, "If only someone would create this," and realized that maybe the idea came to me for a reason—so that I could be the one to bring it to life. Don't sleep on your ideas or dreams, because that vision came into your heart for a reason, and it deserves to be manifested and shared with the world.

Long-Term Vision & Goals

Future Plans

Looking ahead, my next major project is the Mahogany Tarot World Deck. My goal with this deck is to create a truly diverse version of the Rider-Waite deck that still maintains the classic imagery of the backgrounds and symbolism. I want to spread Mahogany Tarot as far and wide as possible, ensuring that those who have been searching for this kind of representation in a tarot deck can find it.

Where I See My Business in 5 to 10 Years

In the next 5 to 10 years, I see myself continuing to sell Mahogany Tarot, both the original and the World Deck, and expanding into other projects that resonate with my passion for healing trauma. I'm currently working on an Oracle deck specifically focused on trauma, as I believe deeply in helping others get to the root of their issues through spiritual tools.

My approach is to stay open to whatever inspirations come to my heart, creating what wants to be created, and putting it out there for others to benefit from. I also plan to start doing more tarot readings, as I want to make sure I'm walking in my purpose and exploring all the ways I can be of service to others on their spiritual journeys.

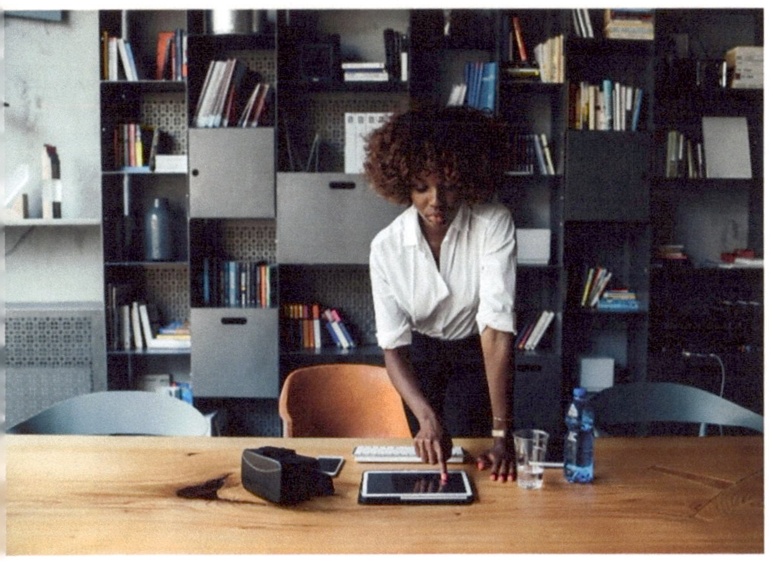

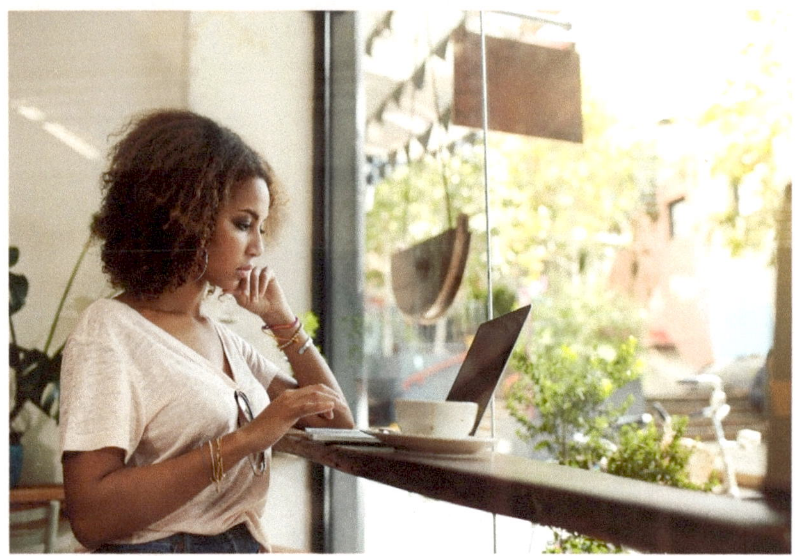

Evolving My Brand

As my business grows, I plan to evolve my brand by continually responding to the needs of the community and the inspirations that come to me. Whether it's through new products, like the trauma-focused Oracle deck, or through expanding the services I offer, I aim to keep my brand aligned with my mission of fostering healing and representation in the spiritual space.

Personal Growth and Development

One of the things that keeps me motivated is the realization of how important it is to help others who are just starting their journey. I've gained so much through my experiences, and I want to share that knowledge to inspire others to see their dreams through. Creating this guide has reminded me of the value in guiding and supporting those who haven't yet been on this path, and it's something I'm passionate about continuing.

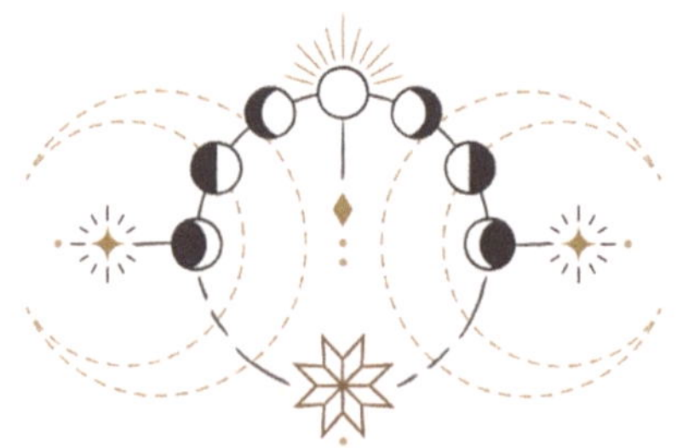

CHAPTER NINE

Final Tips and Advice

Key Takeaways

One of the most important lessons I've learned is that there are people out there waiting for you to create the idea that's in your head. When I created Mahogany Tarot, I didn't realize that so many people had been searching for a deck like mine for years—one that showcases Black people in the classic Tarot style. It's amazing to know that the thing you feel called to create might be exactly what others have been waiting for.

If I could give just one piece of advice, it would be: Just create it. Don't get caught up in the idea of telling others what you're going to do—just focus on the creation itself. When I was working on my deck, I didn't tell anyone; I went into creation mode and only shared it once I had the rough copy in my hand. Getting to the point of having a tangible product is so crucial, and it brings you that much closer to having a solid business where you can actually live off of your sales.

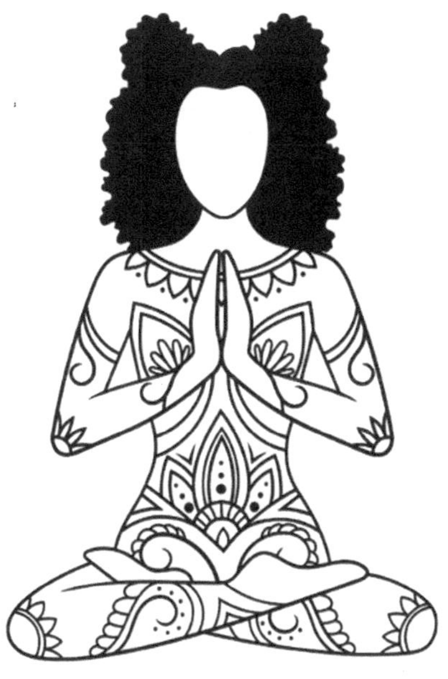

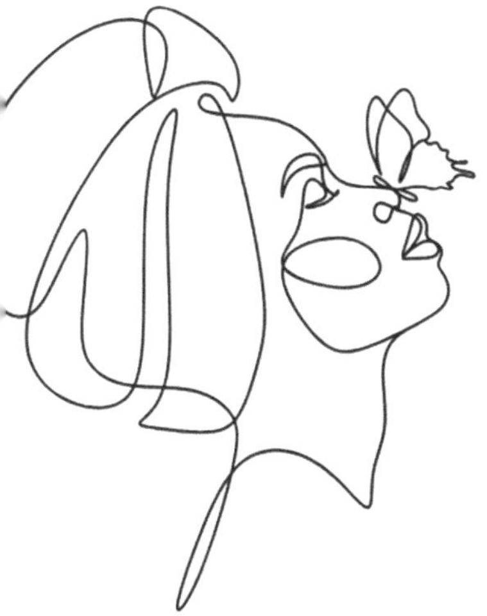

Avoiding Common Pitfalls

A common mistake people make is thinking they need to wait before starting to create. The truth is, creating the product is the most important step. Use your own product, see how you like it, and get real-world feedback. Don't put off creating because of doubts or waiting for the "perfect" time – just get started.

To prepare for challenges, invest in resources like this guide and consume as much relevant content as you can. But don't just consume it- use it. Start applying what you learn right away. Getting started is the key to overcoming those initial hurdles.

Embrace The Journey

If you're feeling overwhelmed, remember that creation is a process. When I was creating my deck, it took me eight months to complete all the cards. Enjoy the process, stay consistent, and pace yourself. You don't have to rush; everything happens in the right timing. As long as you're consistent, you'll eventually reach completion.
It's like working out to achieve a fitness goal—it requires discipline, but if you're creating something you love, that drive will naturally keep you going. When that spark of inspiration hits, start immediately. Don't wait too long, because the excitement can fizzle out. Protect your energy by being mindful of who you share your ideas with. Other people's opinions can sometimes dampen your excitement, so it's important to know yourself and take steps to stay motivated.

For me, not seeking feedback during the initial creation process has been liberating and empowering. I decided to create because I wanted to, not because I needed validation from others. That's my advice to you—just create it, because that vision came into your heart and you are the chosen vessel that will bring it to life. Stay inspired and driven toward creating the projects you want to see in the world. If you're interested in learning more about my journey in creating a tarot deck, I now offer 1-on-1, 30-minute sessions where you can ask me any questions about the process, and I'll guide you through each step. You can purchase these sessions directly through my website. I wish you all the best on your journey and hope that this guide had provided tremendous support.

- KASHEERA HICKSON

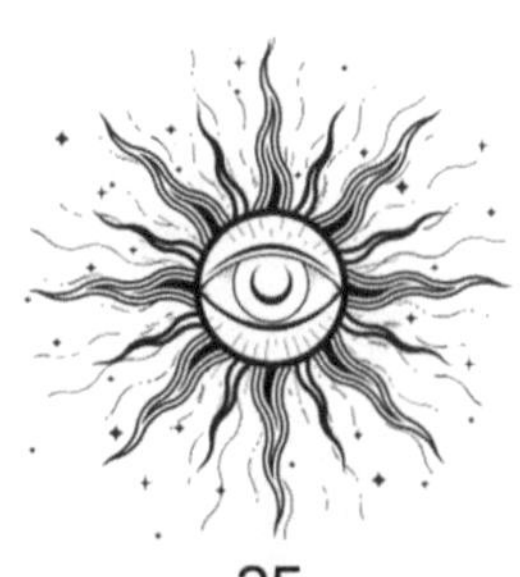

the

CREATE YOUR OWN TAROT DECK GUIDE

IF ANY OF THIS SOUNDS LIKE YOU...

- You've been curious about tarot but never felt confident enough to create your own deck.
- You love expressing yourself through art, but you're unsure where to start or how to bring your ideas to life.
- You want your deck to reflect your personality, culture, and life experiences – not just the traditional designs.
- You've collected tarot decks before, but none have felt fully "yours."
- You wish you had a creative outlet that also deepens your self-awareness and connection to your intuition.

This journal is right for you! It will help you to:

- Turn your tarot vision into a personal, one-of-a-kind deck.
- Gain clarity on the themes, symbols, and colors that inspire you most.
- Develop a deeper understanding of each card's meaning – in your own words.
- Use creative prompts to unlock new ideas and imagery.
- Build confidence in your artistic and intuitive abilities.
- Create a keepsake you can use for readings, meditation, or personal reflection.
- Make space for mindful, relaxing creativity in your life.
- End up with a finished deck that feels authentic and powerful.

HOW TO GET THE MOST OUT OF OF THIS GUIDE

Think of this guide as your creative partner in the journey of bringing your tarot deck to life. You can move through it in order or skip ahead to the prompts that excite you most. I recommend setting aside a quiet, comfortable space where you can work without distractions, and keeping your favorite art supplies nearby.

Start by exploring the foundational prompts that help you define your deck's theme, energy, and inspiration. These pages will guide you to clarify the mood, colors, and symbols that feel most personal to you. Once you have this creative blueprint, move on to the individual card creation pages, focusing on one card at a time.

If possible, dedicate 10–20 minutes a day to your deck. You might sketch, jot down keywords, color in designs, or brainstorm symbols during that time. Over the weeks, you'll see your ideas deepen and your artistic confidence grow.

Don't be afraid to experiment — the beauty of creating your own tarot deck is that there are no strict rules. Allow your imagination to wander, and let your intuition guide your choices. Keep coming back to your earlier pages to see how your vision is evolving.

By the end, you'll have not only the beginnings (or completion) of a tarot deck, but also a visual and written record of your creative process — something you can treasure for years to come.

Prompt 1 – Defining the Essence of Your Deck

Describe your deck as if it already exists in the world.

What is its mood, its personality, and its unique voice?

Does it feel ancient and mysterious, bright and whimsical, bold and revolutionary, or something else entirely?

How would someone feel using it for the first time?

How to Use:
Use your own notebook or sketchbook to explore your ideas for this prompt.

Creative Tip:
Think about how you want people to feel emotionally and physically when they handle your cards for the first time.

How would someone feel using it for the first time?

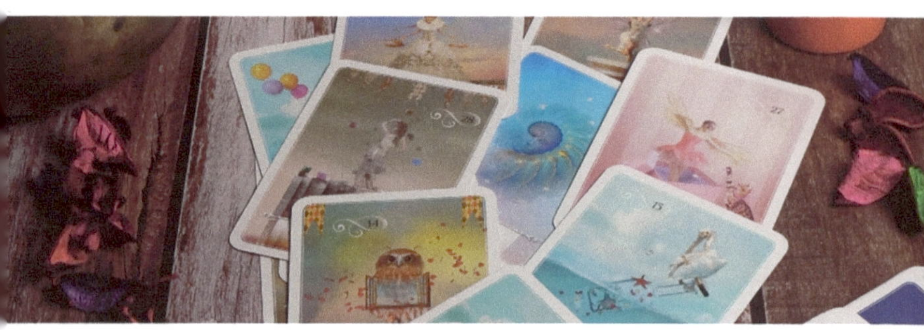

Prompt 2- Gathering Your Inspirations

What inspired you to make this deck in the first place?

List everything – people, experiences, artwork, places, music, books, memories, cultural influences, and spiritual beliefs.

How do these inspirations connect to one another?

Which ones feel essential to include, and which are more subtle influences?

How to Use:
Use your own notebook or sketchbook to explore your ideas for this prompt.

Creative Tip:
Your inspiration list can be a mix of visuals, feelings, and even personal milestones.

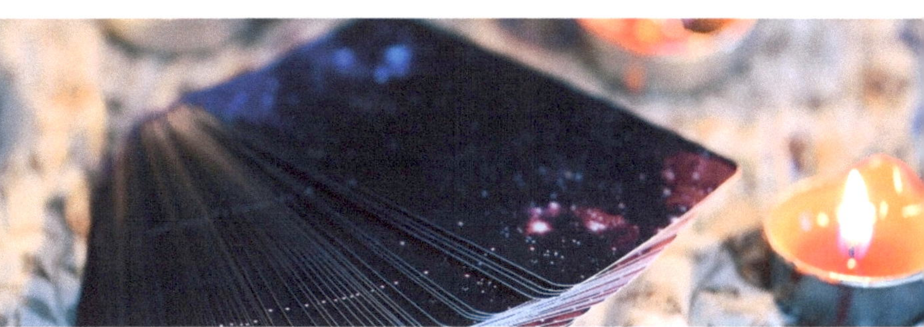

Prompt 3 - The World Your Deck Lives In

If your tarot deck existed as a living, breathing world, what would it look like?

Describe its landscapes, colors, textures, and atmosphere.

What details could you weave into your cards to make that world come alive?

Would it be rooted in nature, cities, dreamscapes, or entirely imagined realms?

How to Use:
Use your own notebook or sketchbook to explore your ideas for this prompt.

Creative Tip:
Consider the climate, lighting, and mood of this world — these can inspire your color palette.

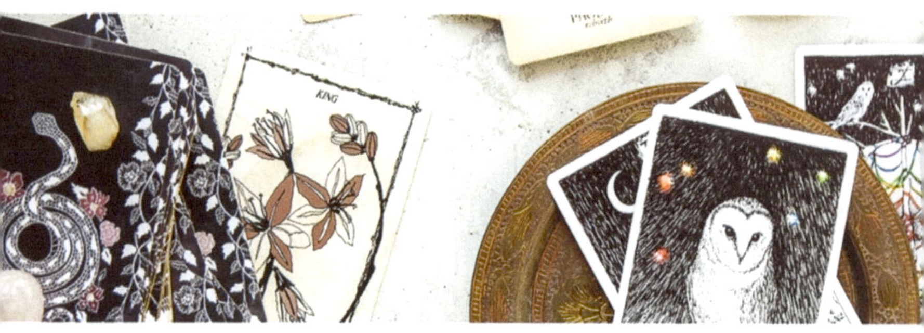

Prompt 4- Building Your Symbol Language

Every tarot deck speaks in symbols — what will yours say?

List the key objects, animals, plants, shapes, and patterns you feel drawn to.

What does each one mean to you personally?

How might these meanings differ from traditional tarot symbolism, and how will that shape your deck's personality?

How to Use:
Use your own notebook or sketchbook to explore your ideas for this prompt.

Creative Tip:
Keep a running list of symbols you love — some may show up in multiple cards.

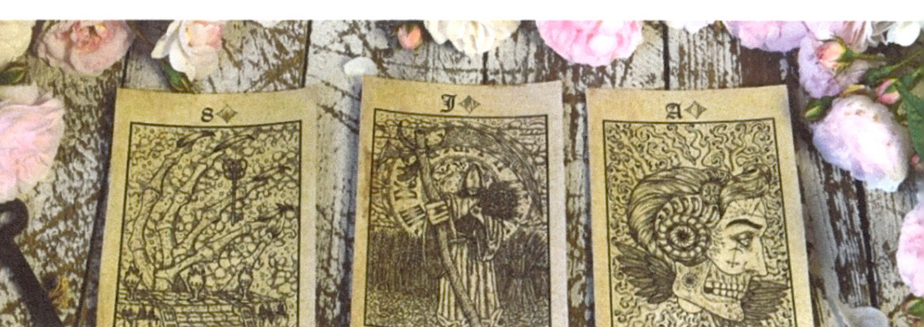

Prompt 5 – Characters, Archetypes & Voices

Think about who or what will embody your Major Arcana, Court Cards, and even the minor cards.

Will they be human, animal, mythical, or a mix?

Describe their personalities, clothing, expressions, and energy.

Are they inspired by real people, fictional characters, or pure imagination?

How to Use:
Use your own notebook or sketchbook to explore your ideas for this prompt.

Creative Tip:
Try writing a short "character bio" for one of your Court Cards.

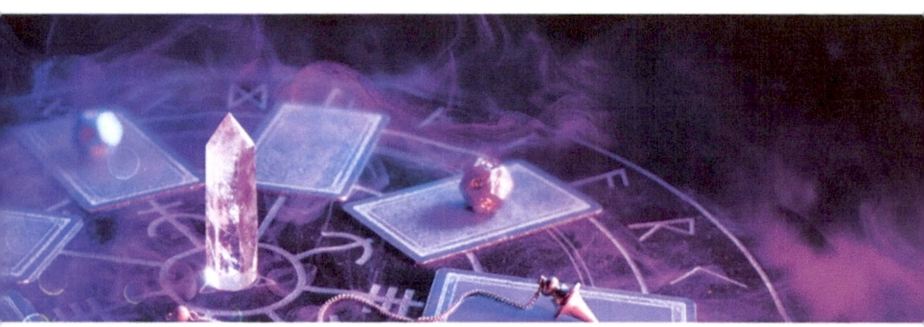

Prompt 6 - Your Deck's Signature Touch

What will make your deck stand out in a sea of tarot decks?

Is it your art style, your cultural perspective, a unique storytelling thread, or completely original card interpretations?

How will this "signature" show up visually and emotionally across the cards?

Describe the feeling someone should get when they realize this deck is unlike any other.

How to Use:
Use your own notebook or sketchbook to explore your ideas for this prompt.

Creative Tip:
Imagine your deck sitting on a store shelf — what would make someone pick it up immediately?

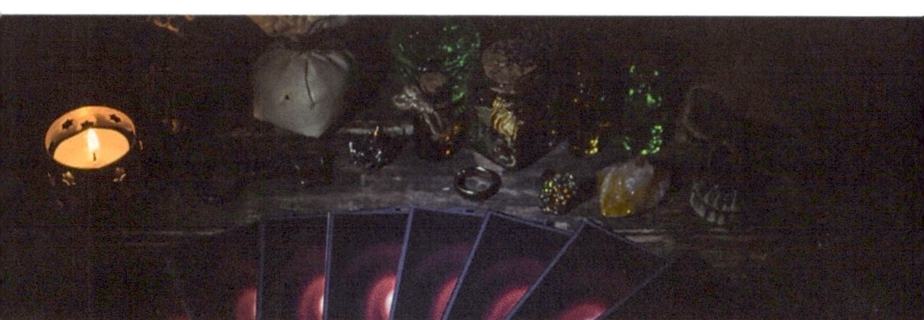

Prompt 7 – Your Deck's Purpose & Legacy

When your deck is finally in someone's hands, what do you want them to experience?

Should it comfort, challenge, inspire, or awaken them?

What personal transformation do you hope it will spark?

Write a vision statement that captures not just the deck's appearance, but its heart and soul.

How to Use:
Use your own notebook or sketchbook to explore your ideas for this prompt.

Creative Tip:
This vision statement can later become part of your deck's marketing description.

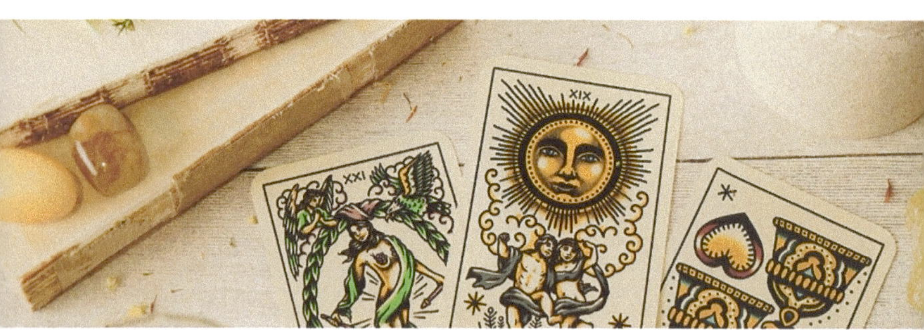

Prompt 8 - Clearing the Path

Every creative journey comes with its own doubts, fears, or roadblocks.

What thoughts or situations might slow you down or stop you from completing your deck?

Be honest — do you worry about your art skills, comparing yourself to other creators, running out of ideas, or finding the time?

For each block you identify, write down one possible solution, shift, or support you can lean on to move forward.

By naming these challenges now, you give yourself the power to navigate them with ease and keep your vision alive.

How to Use:
Use your own notebook or sketchbook to explore your ideas for this prompt.

Creative Tip:
Think of at least one creative ritual that can help you return to your project when you feel stuck.

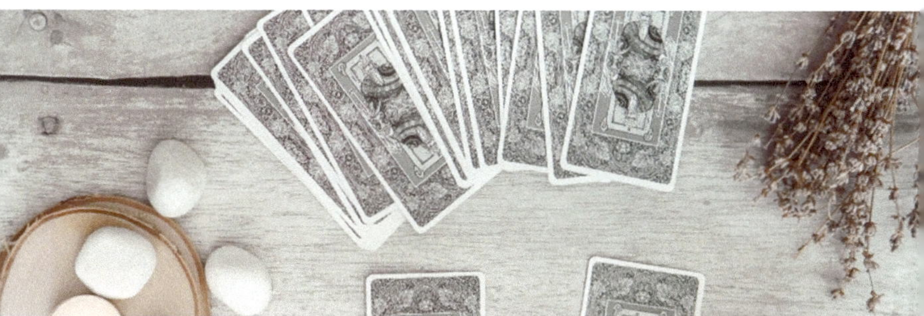

Prompt 9 – Designing the Back of Your Cards

The back of a tarot card is the first thing people see when the deck is face down.

 What feeling or message do you want the back of your cards to convey?

 Should the design be symmetrical so cards can't be identified when reversed?

 What colors, patterns, or symbols feel most aligned with your deck's energy?

How to Use:
Use your own notebook or sketchbook to explore your ideas for this prompt.

Creative Tip:
Consider how your card backs will look when fanned out in a spread — they should feel harmonious and inviting.

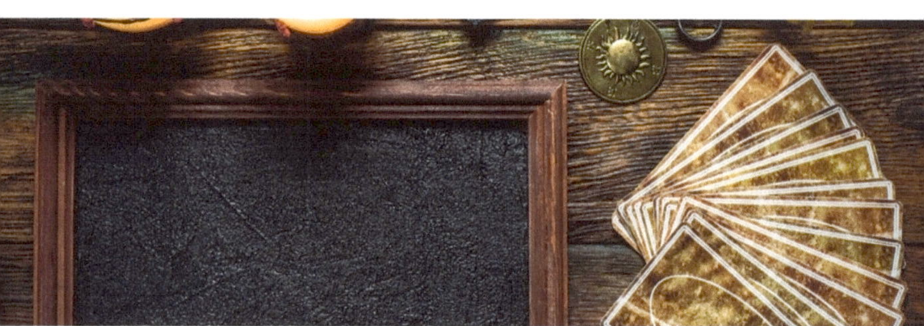

Bonus Prompts:

- What drew you to create your own tarot deck in the first place?
- Which tarot card do you connect with most right now, and why?
- If your deck had a soundtrack, what songs would be on it?
- What season, time of day, or type of weather best matches your deck's mood?
- If you could collaborate with any artist (alive or past) to design one card, who would it be and what would that card look like?
- What everyday object could you turn into a powerful tarot symbol, and what would it mean?
- How would your deck interpret "hope" differently from other decks?
- What card in your deck would be the most surprising or unexpected, and why?
- If your deck had a guardian spirit or guide, who/what would it be?
- How do you want people to feel the first time they hold and shuffle your deck?

How to Use:

Use your own notebook or sketchbook to explore your ideas for this prompt.

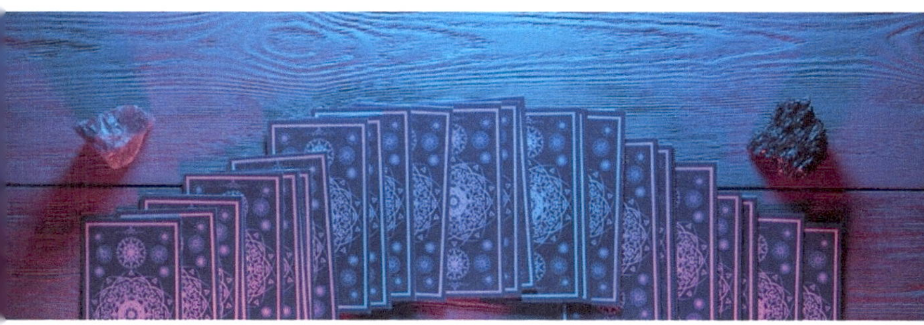

RESOURCES

Promo Materials and Printing:
- **UPrinting: High-quality stickers, thank you cards, and other promo materials.**
- **Visit UPrinting**

Printing Labels:
- **Rollo Printer (from Amazon): Compact and efficient label printer.**
- **Rollo Printer labels on Amazon**

Weighing Packages:
- **Digital Scale (from Amazon): Accurate scale for weighing shipments.**
- **Digital Scale on Amazon**

Boxes and Packaging:
- **The Boxery (purchased through eBay): Affordable boxes for shipping.**
- **The Boxery**

Packing Paper:
- **Packing Paper (from Amazon): Durable packing paper to protect your decks.**
- **Packing Paper on Amazon**

Tissue Paper:
- **Tissue Paper: Currently sourced from Ross, looking for a wholesale retailer.**

Design and Creation Tools:
- **Photoshop: Industry-standard software for creating and editing artwork.**
- **Visit Photoshop**
- **MidJourney: AI tool for generating creative artwork.**
- **Visit MidJourney**
- **DALL·E: AI tool for generating realistic images based on prompts.**
- **Visit DALL·E**

Website and E-commerce Platforms:
- **Shopify: Create and manage your online store.**
- **Visit Shopify**
- **GoDaddy: Domain registration and hosting services.**
- **Visit GoDaddy**

Manufacturing and Sourcing:
- **Print Ninja: High-quality printing services with a handy cost calculator.**
- **Visit Print Ninja**
- **Alibaba: Sourcing manufacturers and suppliers.**
- **Visit Alibaba**

E-commerce and Marketing:
- **Etsy: Marketplace for selling handmade products.**
- **Visit Etsy**
- **Amazon: Marketplace for selling products, including tarot decks.**
- **Visit Amazon**

RESOURCES

SEO and Marketing Tools:
- eRank: SEO tool for Etsy sellers.
- Visit eRank
- Google Keyword Planner: Tool for keyword research.
- Visit Google Keyword Planner
- Instagram: Social media platform for marketing.
- Visit Instagram
- TikTok: Social media platform for marketing.
- Visit TikTok

Accounting and Finances:
- QuickBooks: Accounting software for small businesses.
- Visit QuickBooks
- Wells Fargo: Business checking and credit card services.
- Visit Wells Fargo
- Navy Federal Credit Union: Banking and credit services.
- Visit Navy Federal Credit Union

Customer Service and Shipping:
- Pirate Ship: Affordable shipping solutions for small businesses.
- Visit Pirate Ship

Additional Resources and Tools

Design Tools:
- Prompt Base: Platform for purchasing AI-generated prompts for creating specific styles of artwork.
- Visit Prompt Base

Graphic Design Software:
- Affinity: Affordable graphic design software as an alternative to Photoshop.
- Visit Affinity
- GIMP: Free and open-source image editor, great for those on a budget.
- Visit GIMP
- Procreate: Powerful illustration app for iPad, ideal for artists.
- Visit Procreate